BIRDS

PARTS OF AN
ANIMAL

Written by Emilie Dufresne

PHOTO CREDITS

Front Cover – Sergey Uryadnikov, Narupan Nimpaiboon, Ismael Jorda, Anna Kaewkhammul, Nomad_Soul, Martin Mecnarowski, Teri virickis, 2 – Edwin Godinho, 3 – janniwet, 4 – Jim Nelson, 5 – Gallinago_media, paula french, yoshio511, 6 – Milan Zygmunt, 7 – Gelpi, Bobeh, BananyakoSensei, 8 – Guoqiang Xue, 9 –Usagi-P, sen yang, 10 – Ondrej Prosicky, 11 – Carol Gray, 12 – FotoRequest, 13 – aaltair, 14 – Lukas Bornheim, 15 – Paolo-mazi, 16 – Kurit afshen, 17 – Sumruay Rattanataipob, 18 –Dr Steven Murray, 19 – Nuki Sharir, 20 – MZPHOTO.CZ, 21 – BlueOrange Studio, 22 –Purino, 23 – Wildlife World, Anthony Smith Images, Agnieszka Bacal, Belen Bilgic Schneider.

Images are courtesy of Shutterstock.com. With thanks to Getty Images, Thinkstock Photo and iStockphoto.

BookLife
PUBLISHING

©2018
Book Life
King's Lynn
Norfolk PE30 4LS

ISBN: 978-1-78637-431-8

Written by:
Emilie Dufresne

Edited by:
Kirsty Holmes

Designed by:
Amy Li

BIRDS

Words that look like **this** can be found in the glossary on page 24.

WHAT IS A BIRD?

There are so many animals in the world that we split them into different **categories**. This helps us tell all of the animals apart.

One of these categories is birds.

Penguin

Ostrich

Swallow

There are lots of different kinds of birds; those that fly, those that run, and those that swim.

HOW DO YOU KNOW?

We can ask certain questions to find out if an animal is a bird or not.

How do we know that

this is a bird?

CHECKLIST

Does it have feathers? ✓

Does it lay hard-shelled eggs? ✓

Does it have a beak? ✓

Does it have wings? ✓

IT'S A BIRD!

HEADS AND SHOULDERS

Some birds can turn their heads so that they are looking behind them. This lets them see almost all around them.

FIND **OUT** MORE **ABOUT** MY EYES ON PAGE 12!

Wrist

Elbow

Shoulder

Birds don't have arms like humans; they have wings instead. Wings have three **joints** just like a human arm: the shoulder, the elbow and the wrist.

KNEES AND TOES

Birds have knees just like humans, but they aren't where you expect them to be. The joint this flamingo is bending is its ankle!

CAN'T... REACH. MUST... SCRATCH CHIN.

Birds' knees are hidden by their feathers.

The bald eagle's curved talons are specially

adapted for landing in trees.

Birds have claws at the end of their toes. If these claws are very long and sharp, they are called talons.

EYES AND EARS

Birds have even better sight than humans. They can focus on different objects very quickly and they can even see **ultraviolet** light. This helps them easily spot berries hidden by **foliage**.

This is how a bird sees.

Birds have similar hearing to humans. Birds are particularly good at recognising different noises and where they are coming from. Their ears are hidden by feathers.

MOUTH AND NOSE

Instead of a mouth, birds have beaks. Birds use their beaks for digging, pecking and eating. Beaks are all different shapes and sizes.

Hummingbirds have long thin beaks so that

they can drink nectar from flowers.

Most birds rely on their hearing and sight, because they can't smell very well. Vultures, however, can smell their food from

SKIN

Birds have two layers of feathers covering their skin; an outer layer and an inner layer of **down**. This helps to protect them and keep them warm.

Have you ever noticed that most birds don't have feathers on their legs? This part of a bird has scaly skin, like you would find on **reptiles**.

BIRDS THAT BREAK THE RULES

All birds have wings and feathers, but not all birds can fly.
These penguins can't fly (or walk very well) but they
are great swimmers!

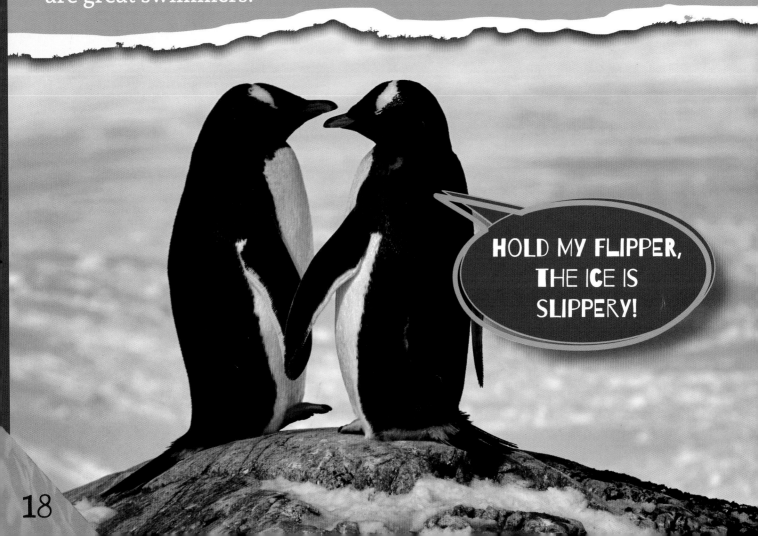

HOLD MY FLIPPER,
THE ICE IS
SLIPPERY!

Albatrosses fly

using **dynamic soaring**.

Some birds can't fly, whilst others barely stop flying.
An albatross can fly around the whole world in around
50 days! They only have to flap their wings every few hours.

BRILLIANT BIRDS

These blue-footed boobies have, as the name suggests, bright blue feet! They dance and show off their feet to the other birds.

Male peacocks have a long **train** of feathers with blue and green patterns on them. This peacock is showing off his feathers by spreading them out like a fan.

ACTIVITY

Do you have a garden or a park near your house? You could go and count how many different types of bird you can see.

Take a parent or guardian with you to help **identify** the birds.

Starling

Robin

Duck

Grebe

Here are some birds you might see!

GLOSSARY

ADAPTED	changed over time to suit the environment
CATEGORIES	different sections within a larger group
DOWN	a layer of small, fluffy feathers underneath a bird's outer feathers
DYNAMIC SOARING	a type of flying where a bird glides across different air pockets, rather than flap its wings
FOLIAGE	a group of plants or leaves
IDENTIFY	spot or recognise
JOINTS	moveable place where two bones are connected
REPTILES	cold-blooded animals with scales
TRAIN	the back part of a peacock's body that is made of very long feathers
ULTRAVIOLET	a type of light that only some animals can see that helps them see their environment better

INDEX